Baysic History Trail

A View From the Water

by
Lillie Gilbert,
Belinda Nash
&
Deni Norred-Williams

For my good friend and fellow water-lover — SYOTR Lillie

Virginia Beach, Virginia

Copyright © 2003 Bayside Researchers

Published by:
ECO IMAGES
Virginia Beach, Virginia

ISBN: 0-938423-09-6

Available from:
Bayside Researchers
3636 Virginia Beach Blvd., #108
Virginia Beach, VA 23452
www.wildriveroutfitters.com
757.431.8566

All rights reserved, including the right of reproduction in whole or in part in any form or by any means, electronic or mechanical.

Printed in the United States of America

First Printing

Louisa Venable Kyle on the occasion of her 94th birthday, 1997

Photo by Belinda Nash

*This book is dedicated to the memory of
Louisa Venable Kyle,
historian, storyteller, writer, gracious lady
and friend to all who knew her.*

*"Without a cultural history,
people are rootless.
Preserving remnants offers lingering evidence to
remind people of
what they once were, who they are,
what they are and where they are."*

– John L. Crompton

Table of Contents

Foreword	*viii*
Preface	*x*
Acknowledgements	*xi*
Introduction	*xii*
Part 1: Lynnhaven River and Lynnhaven Bay	15
Description	16
History of the Lynnhaven	19
The Opening of Lynnhaven Inlet	21
Even Before That	23
Bounty of the Land and Water	24
Part 2: Boating Access to the Western Branch of the Lynnhaven River	29
Lynnhaven Boat and Beach Facility	30
Part 3: Destinations	33
Destination 1. Pleasure House Creek	34
Bayville Manor House	37
History of the Lynnhaven Oyster	38
Morning Star Baptist Church	41
Destination 2. Church Point	42
History of the Courthouses	44
Towns on the Rivers	46
Little Neck	47
Destination 3. Thoroughgood Cove	50
Adam Thoroughgood	50
John Gookin's Landing	52
Destination 4. Witch Duck Bay	54
Grace Sherwood	55

Kayaking into History	57
The Chapel at Haygood United Methodist Church	58
Lynnhaven House	59
Old Donation Episcopal Church	61
Ferry Plantation House	64
The Lynnhaven Ferry System	65
White Acres	67
Destination 5. Thurston Branch	69
History of Thurston Branch/Bennetts Creek	69
Destination 6. Thalia Creek	71
History of Thalia Creek	73
History of Timber Necke and Pembroke	76
German Prisoner of War Camp	78

Afterword	79
Essentials for Paddlers/Boaters	80
What to Wear	81
Boating Safety	82
More Information	83
References	84
Helpful Resources	88
Index	92
About the Authors	96

Foreword

Bayside History Trail: A View from the Water is intended to inform readers about historical aspects of Princess Anne County/Virginia Beach; to provide a new perspective on the past through a view from the water which also emphasizes environmental change; and to entertain through stories which hint at the lives of folk who occupied the Lynnhaven over the centuries. The three authors bring to their task years of experience as teachers, storytellers, researchers, and lovers of the waterways.

The authors have been careful to acknowledge that the sources historians have available range from the well documented to the highly anecdotal, and they consistently have avoided accepting the anecdotal as fact. The reader therefore can rely upon the factual statements while enjoying tales which likely have been embellished with the retelling over time.

Since Princess Anne County residents from the seventeenth century into the twentieth relied heavily, at times almost exclusively, upon water routes for internal transportation the thought of viewing land sites from the water is creative and appropriate. This approach has its challenges, as the authors note, since the shorelines have constantly changed over time, but again they have been judicious in accepting questionable claims about current shoreline configurations.

Whether readers board canoes and traverse the Lynnhaven with this volume in hand, or imagine the water-to-shore perspective from their armchairs, *Bayside History Trail: A View From the Water* will confirm the resourcefulness and creativity of our ancestors; demonstrate how much insight into the past we can extract from structures and sites which have survived; and remind us of the broader historical impact of Southeast Virginia.

The many of us who played some role in the development of the Bayside History Trail concept have been gratified by the public's response to the linkage of the sites along the Trail, and this book offers an engaging way of making the Trail even more useful and meaningful.

Stephen Mansfield
Virginia Wesleyan College

Preface

While most people prefer to visit historical areas by land, a **view from the water** puts the visitor at an eye-level most appreciated by the early settlers. Waterways were vital to the developing communities of the New World and represented all aspects of life, not just commerce and travel.

The view from the water of the many coves of the Lynnhaven offers boaters a unique opportunity to understand the geographic importance of the placement of the early structures for safety from storms, ease of commerce and travel by water, and the necessity of the early ferries that transported people and goods from the eastern and western sides of the Lynnhaven River. Understand that this is largely a virtual tour as the shoreline has changed radically and the only structures visible today from the water that are described in this book are Bayville Manor House, Ferry Plantation House, and Steinhilber's Thalia Acres Inn. An elderly tree of historical interest and remnants of an old cypress log bridge dating back to the 1700s are visible from the water as well.

It is our hope that this book will be carried by boating travelers to enhance the journey down the historic and vital Western Branch of the Lynnhaven River in Virginia Beach, VA. If the reader is not a boater, it is hoped that this book will offer a new way to view our historic community. Enjoy!

Acknowledgements

Thank you to all of the people who are supporters of historical structures in Virginia Beach. We appreciate your efforts more than you will ever know Thanks are way past due to all of the early writers and recorders of our local history. Without the energy and appreciation of the past exhibited in the years of collections, recollections, photographs, and recordings, we would have no book to share.

To all of the canoeists and kayakers who have shown an interest in more than just a cursory look at our waterways, we thank you for your support and conservation efforts.

– Lillie, Belinda, Deni

Introduction

The original Bayside History Trail, dedicated in 1999, is a land route connecting a series of roads and walkways that lead to ten significant historical sites. It is located near the Western Branch of the Lynnhaven Bay and Lynnhaven River. The **trail from the water** designates various sites of historical importance to the development of Virginia Beach from colonial times to the present.

The settlement of colonists in the area we now call Virginia Beach was centered close to the water. In fact, the early roadways were old animal trails, Native American trails, or waterways. The term "Hampton Roads" referred not to roads on land but waterways. On a French map of our area drawn in 1781, "Rade D'Hampton" is clearly shown as the waterway between present-day Hampton and Willoughby. Closer to our area, the term "Lynnhaven Roads" is indicated on several old maps. The "Roads" that were more protected waterways also refer to areas where ships could ride safely at anchor (Hampton Roads Chamber of Commerce, 1999).

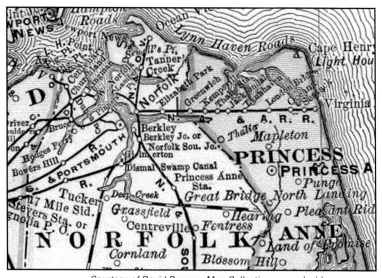

Courtesy of David Rumsey Map Collection, www.davidrumsey.com

The colonists could get around more easily by water and situated their churches, houses and farms with boat landings along protected waterways. Plantation houses were seldom more than 100 to 150 feet from a waterway. Indeed, many of the families along the Lynnhaven built their homes on wooded points of the river. Said Whichard (1959), "… people built their homes facing the streams on which they settled. Nearly every settler had his skiff or shallop in which he could row or sail to church, to court, to market, and in going about his other business and social activities."

We are fortunate to have a number of colonial and pre-1900 structures still in use in Virginia Beach. Located along the Western Branch of the Lynnhaven the remaining early homes open to the public are the Adam Thoroughgood House, circa 1680, the Lynnhaven House, 1725, and the Ferry Plantation House, circa 1830. The early churches are Old Donation Episcopal Church from 1736, Morning Star Baptist Church founded in 1892, and The Chapel at Haygood United Methodist Church, 1896. The only private home that we are listing is Bayville Manor House because it is visible from the water. Pembroke Manor House, 1764, also presented in this book, is available for tours by appointment only. These represent a fraction of what was built along the thriving waterway and adjacent land.

Part One

Lynnhaven River
&
Lynnhaven Bay

Lynnhaven River & Lynnhaven Bay

"Lynnhaven Bay is a portion of the Chesapeake, at its southern extremity, and lies between Cape Henry and a point at Little Creek Inlet. The waters of the Chesapeake here make a graceful curve into the land; and the view, to the north especially, is extensive, and very beautiful. Lynnhaven River is, also, a truly beautiful collection of water, which extends into Princess Anne County from the bay."

– William S. Forrest, 1853

Description

The historic Lynnhaven River, a tidal tributary of the southern Chesapeake Bay, flows past many stately homes that line it and the historic Lynnhaven Bay. Lynnhaven Bay is formed by the Eastern and Western Branches of the Lynnhaven River, which empty into it. This book will focus on the Western Branch of the Lynnhaven River.

Chrissie Harney and Zak Montoya at Lynnhaven Boat and Beach Facility

Photo by Lillie Gilbert

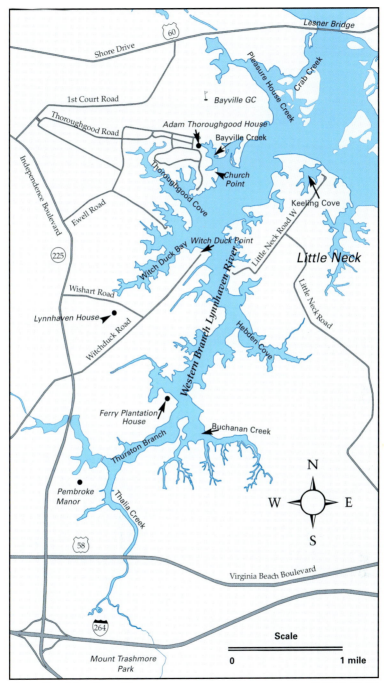

Western Branch Lynnhaven River

River depths of the Western Branch vary between 2 to 20 feet at mean low water. The dredged channels vary from 6 to 12 feet at mean low water. The longest fetch of the Western Branch is from Lesner Bridge to Witch Duck Point. It offers a spectacular view of this part of the Lynnhaven, one steeped in history as the reader will discover. This branch of the historic river is approximately 6 miles in length and covers approximately 1,000 acres. The shoreline is composed of fringe marsh and artificially stabilized shore. There are a few sand beaches, but no designated swimming areas. The only public boating access site is at the Lynnhaven Boat and Beach Facility located at Crab Creek near the opening of the Lynnhaven River to the Chesapeake Bay.

Photo by Lillie Gilbert

Lynnhaven Boat and Beach Facility information kiosk, boardwalk trail and kayak launch area

History of the Lynnhaven

The Lynnhaven Bay and its river with two branches were named early on during the English settlements. Local historians say that Adam Thoroughgood (1602-1640), one of our area's first settlers, named the Lynnhaven after the area in England from whence he came. The land in this northern portion of what was to become Virginia Beach was known as Linhaven Parish of Lower Norfolk when Elizabeth City Shire (County) was divided in 1638. A 1651 map of Virginia Farrer shows the "Lin haven" River. Virginia's father, John Farrer, was an investor in the Virginia Company of London. This is the company that had been given a royal charter to colonize between the 34th and 45th parallels in the New World. The 1651 map is notable, not only in that it names the "Lin haven," but that it locates the Sea of China and the Indies just over what later would be called the Blue Ridge Mountains.

Ten years before Virginia Farrer's map was completed, Sir William Berkeley boarded a ship bound for the colony. He brought with him the King's commission as a royal governor of Virginia and he held this office intermittently for thirty-five years. When he arrived in February of 1642 the colony consisted of "8,000 sickly souls," but by the end of Berkeley's tenure in 1677 Virginia's population had risen to 40,000 (Fischer and Kelly, 2000).

In the early years of the settlement along the Lynnhaven River, all court proceedings took place at the church with the vestry as jurors. It was the wish of the Crown that the Virginia colony set up churches and courthouses close to each other. In 1661 the first courthouse in Lower Norfolk County was built on the waterfront at Broad Creek. With the population spreading, in 1689 two courthouses replaced the first one, also close to water, as the rivers were the easiest travel routes before formal roads were built and maintained. These new courthouses were on the Elizabeth River and Wolfsnare Creek off the Eastern Branch of the Lynnhaven River. In 1695 the Court moved to the western shoreline of the Lynnhaven River, "its timbers hauled by boat and cart" (Whichard, 1959) to the grounds of the Ferry Farm location next to the Old Donation Church. It was not until 1986 that the remains of the second courthouse (in what is now Virginia Beach) were discovered by local archaeologist Floyd Painter.

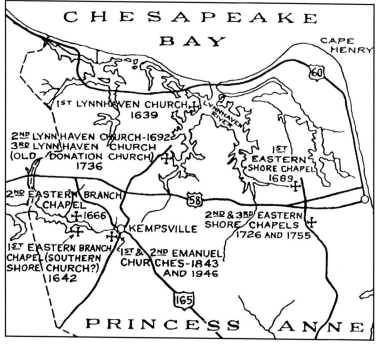

Map of Princess Anne County, showing colonial church sites transcribed by George C. Mason, *The Colonial Vestry Book of Lynnhaven Parish, Princess Anne County, Virginia, 1723-1786.*

> *Rivers must have been the guides which conducted the footsteps of the first travelers. They are the constant lure, when they flow by our doors, to distant enterprise and adventure, and, by a natural impulse, the dwellers on their banks will at length accompany their currents to the lowlands of the globe, or explore at their invitation the interior of continents.*
>
> – Henry David Thoreau

The Opening of Lynnhaven Inlet

The accounts of Bishop William Meade (1857) contend that the Lynnhaven River initially followed a long, narrow estuary and flowed into the Chesapeake Bay at Little Creek. This theory, truth, or legend - for it does have its skeptics - further asserts that the present Lynnhaven Inlet was artificially opened by the area's seine-haulers for their ease of access to fishing grounds. As the story goes, fishermen dug a trench across a half-mile sandbar some time in the mid 1600s in order to prevent a six-mile trip by water to the Chesapeake Bay shore. Meade quotes an unnamed source as follows:

> ... the people ... gathered their hands together, and, with their field-hoes, opened a trench across the beach wide enough to admit the passage of a canoe, not dreaming of any consequences beyond their immediate object.

The consequences referred to were of amazing, if not historic proportions: the trench was purportedly widened quickly and considerably by the rushing in of an "invasion of waters ... piled up by an easterly wind from the Atlantic." Meade's teller further asserted that the land flooded as far as London Bridge six miles away, thereby forming "in their mad career " the new mouth of the Lynnhaven, drastically and forever changing the river's course. In so doing, the waters swept away "nearly the whole of the burying-ground attached to the church" (the parish's first, at Church Point) and separated the church from its glebe lands. The erosion, whether immediate or gradual, prompted the building of a second church, which was completed in 1692.

Painting by John White, 1585-86

Even before that...

Floyd Painter also dug up, so to speak, the history of the **Chesapeake Indians** native to this area more than a staggering 2,000 years ago. This tribe of Algonquian linguistic stock inhabited the estuarine region bordered by the Lynnhaven and Broad Bays. The Chesapeans roamed the banks of saltwater and freshwater rivers, bays, and marshes. They sustained themselves and their families from, in addition to small game and wildfowl, the Lynnhaven River's bountiful supply of fish and oysters. They gathered the then-plentiful oysters from shallow waters at low tide, perhaps with feet swaddled in tough animal hides, as did the Nanticoke Indians, their contemporary gatherers of the bivalve. The Chesapeans probably fished using several methods, one being with weir fences made of woven reeds and rushes; these guided fish into mazes ending in holding pens, in which the swimmers became trapped. Another method of fishing was to burn a fire at night in the pit of one's canoe and spear the fish when the luminosity of the fire lured them to surface. Sharp shells or fish teeth sometimes tipped the Native Americans' arrows and spears (Egloff & Woodward, 1992). The stone projectile points which have been found in abundance here are trade items, as there is no native stone in this immediate area.

Some historians believe that Chief Powhatan exterminated the Chesapeake Indians sometime before 1612. Long since eradicated, there are no living descendants of the Chesapeake Indians today. One can visit the re-interment site of 64 tribe members, however, at First Landing State Park in Virginia Beach, VA (Waugaman & Moretti-Langholtz, 2000).

Bounty of the Land and Water

Our local waters, salt or brackish, provided a wide array of animal and plant life useful to the Native Americans and later to the colonists. Native Americans who lived in the Bayside area are believed to have been largely hunters and gatherers as the coastal marshes provided an abundance of game, fish, and shellfish. The uplands provided nuts, fruits, roots, and seeds. A great number of stone tools and pottery shards have been found, indicating trade with others and, more than likely, established seasonal villages or camps.

Projectile points found on the Western Branch of the Lynnhaven River at Thoroughgood Point. These have been identified: (1) Late Archaic/Early Woodland Period, 3500 BC-0 AD; (2) Woodland Period, 1000 BC-1000 AD.

When John White and Thomas Hariot from England explored the area in 1585-6, they stayed part of the time with the Chesapeans and reported two villages between the Eastern and Western Branches of the Lynnhaven River. White drew a map of the area labeling one of these villages "Apasus" (Rountree, 1996). As white settlers moved in, they found the bounty of the land and water to their liking, as well. The blue crab, clams, mussels and oysters provided wonderful meals as well as substantial income for those who later mastered the harvesting techniques. Salt could be easily procured by evaporative processes.

Eggs from nesting birds were another edible benefit of coastal living. The settlers collected bird eggs, as did generations of coastal dwellers. Until federal law banned this activity, wimbrels, clapper rails, and gulls lost many an egg (Badger,

1996). From wills of the wealthier colonists with family shipping and mercantile businesses, it is apparent that feathers from wild birds such as ducks, turkeys, and swans were gathered for feather beds (Turner, 1984). By the later colonial period and throughout the 1800s, before the days when game hunting was controlled, the county became known for its large turkeys, wild ducks, geese, and quail (Kyle, 1964).

Native Americans in Tidewater long preceded the colonists in their use of the land for subsistence and they provided the early settlers with a good example. In this area, corn, beans and squash were among the Chesapeans' agricultural staples. From records, we know that fruit trees flourished along the banks of the Lynnhaven River: John Saunders of Pembroke Plantation had "two apple orchards of more than seven hundred bearing trees" (*The Beach*, 1996). Prompted by the dream of the London Company that Virginia replace the Orient in the manufacturing of silk, King Charles II ordered the colonists to plant imported white mulberry trees, "ten to be planted every 100 acres" (silkworms feed on their leaves). Although they failed at the silkworm/mulberry effort, the colonists were successful with another insect's product and collected much beeswax and honey (Turner, 1984). Not heeding history's lesson on the silkworm, county residents two centuries later, in the 1830s, revitalized their efforts with the Asian insect and again failed (Mansfield, 1989).

These failures aside, there are many useful plants that are still growing in the Lynnhaven area that were used by the colonists. Several of them are described here. An edible, small succulent plant is saltwort, *Salicornia* spp. The little segmented pieces of the plant could easily be broken off, boiled, and combined with vinegar and spices to provide a tasty relish. Saltwort can be eaten raw, but is fairly salty. Waxmyrtle bushes provided seeds with a waxy coating that could be boiled off and the wax collected for candle making. Bayberry candles are the gently scented result. Colonists learned to appreciate many of the Lauraceous or other plants that had conspicuously

Crop land at Bayville Manor, early 1970s   *Courtesy of Calvert Lester*

aromatic fruits, bark, leaves, or roots, sassafras being another example (Whichard, 1959).

In time, as more land was cleared, colonial farms and plantations provided cultivated crops for local consumption and commercial use. As centuries of tobacco growing had depleted nutrients from the soils, subsequent crops included corn, potatoes, oats, wheat, and, to a lesser extent, cotton (Mansfield, 1989). Hops were also grown, and in the 18th century homemade beer and cider were perfected and replaced imported liquor in the local taverns (Turner, 1984). Produce for export or for the market was loaded directly from the property holder's land, as most of the farms were located near the water's edge.

Generally flat-bottom boats or large canoes were used to

HMS Challenger, 1880   Courtesy of NOAA/Dept. of Commerce, 1800

transport goods from shallower waters to deeper parts of the river or to Lynnhaven Inlet and Chesapeake Bay where products were loaded onto larger vessels for commercial purposes. Transport was much easier by water as the early roads were few, eroded easily by rains and difficult to build and maintain. From the 1890s through relatively recent days, truck farming became quite prevalent in the mild-climated Princess Anne County. Fruits and vegetables were produced and sent to northern markets (Kyle, 1964).

Old Flat-bottom oyster boat   Courtesy of John W. Keeling

Part Two

*Boating Access
to the
Western Branch
of the
Lynnhaven River*

Boating Access to the Western Branch of the Lynnhaven River

Lynnhaven Boat and Beach Facility on Crab Creek off Shore Drive (U.S. 60) at the Lesner Bridge, Virginia Beach, VA. By boat, mileage variable, round trip suggested. Descriptions of paddling destinations follow.

Canoe/Kayak Access: *Lynnhaven Boat and Beach Facility* off Shore Drive (US 60) and Stratford Road, southwest of the Lesner Bridge. The access site for canoes and kayaks is the sandy beach area to the west of the double boat ramps for motorized craft. This small sandy beach is near the first parking area when entering the facility. The Lynnhaven Boat and Beach Facility, completed in November of 2001, is a very well-planned access site with many conveniences. There are restrooms with shower and foot rinse areas, changing rooms, an

Courtesy of Public Works/Beach Management, City of Virginia Beach, VA

information desk, vending machines, and a boardwalk leading to the Ocean Park Beach Area located on the Chesapeake Bay. There are parking fees for non-motorized craft that are cartopped and ramp fees for trailered boats. The site is open 24 hours a day, 7 days a week. If paddling, be aware of motorized craft, as this is a shared channel leading into Lynnhaven River.

The Bayside History Trail by water does not extend into the Chesapeake Bay and we do not advise paddling through Lynnhaven Inlet under the Lesner Bridge. As a precautionary note, the currents under the Lesner Bridge are treacherous. Many swimmers have lost their lives here. On a historical note, the original **Lesner Bridge** was a drawbridge built in 1928 and named for State Senator John A. Lesner of Norfolk. It was replaced in 1958 by a stationary bridge. Currently there are twin stationary bridges.

Photo by Lillie Gilbert

Lynnhaven Boat and Beach Facility with paddlers disembarking at the sandy beach area across from the paved boat ramps, access points for motorized craft

Part Three

Destinations

Destinations

Destination 1: *Pleasure House Creek*

An easy paddle if one has just a few hours is to put in at Crab Creek and take a right out of the narrow canal into a salt marsh and continue into **Pleasure House Creek** to the west. This area is too shallow for motor boats and is recommended for canoes and kayaks only. Pleasure House Creek, Pleasure House Point, Pleasure House Road and the former Pleasure House Beach derive their name from a tavern from the 1770s, which was located near the beach until sometime in the 1800s.

One of the great pleasures today in this immediate area is

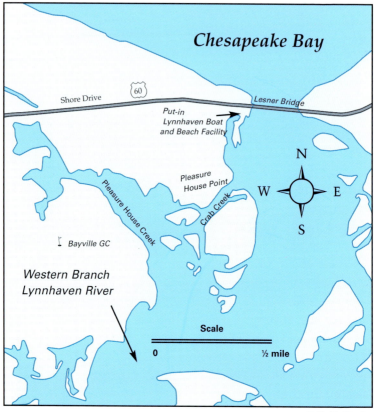

© Vickie Shufer

for birders who explore the many salt marshes. Even on a windy day, one can find refuge in the waters near the **Bayville Golf Club**, completed in 1997 on property that used to be **Bayville Dairy Farms**.

Photos by Lillie Gilbert

View of barns from the water

Visible from the water are the roofs of two very large barns that replaced the older ones that served the dairy. These new barns were built to preserve the "farm feel" and are now utilized by the golf club for storage. The clubhouse, which opened on Labor Day of 2001, can also be seen from the water.

From the water the golf course is barely visible from a canoe or kayak. It is enjoyable to explore the many small waterways that wind through the cordgrass. To this day, the birding and fishing are good, but the area is off-limits for shellfish. The days of the famous Lynnhaven oyster are unfortunately past. In 1998 attempts to revive some of the oyster grounds in the Lynnhaven were initiated by the Virginia Institute of Marine Science and the Chesapeake Bay

Foundation. This project is to remain in place for several years with volunteers maintaining each site. If you happen to paddle near some of the artificial oyster reefs, please do not disturb them. For information, go to *http://www.vims.edu/mullusc/*.

Pleasure House Cove is remembered by Lillie Gilbert as being an area where hundreds of small sea turtles were once swimming in the water.

> *It was sometime in the late 1970s when Nancy Andrews and I were canoeing at the mouth of Pleasure House Cove not far from Crab Creek. Ahead of us were what appeared to be hundreds of small, black, pyramid-shaped bobbing objects. As the canoe floated through them, we realized that they were little turtles! We have never seen anything like this since.*

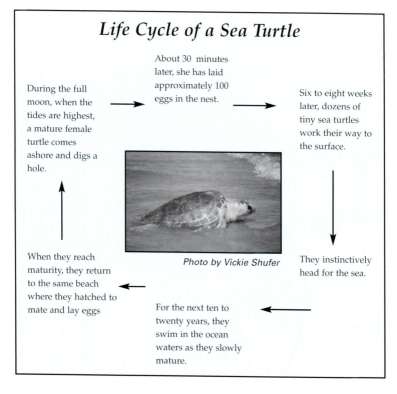

Life Cycle of a Sea Turtle

During the full moon, when the tides are highest, a mature female turtle comes ashore and digs a hole.

About 30 minutes later, she has laid approximately 100 eggs in the nest.

Six to eight weeks later, dozens of tiny sea turtles work their way to the surface.

Photo by Vickie Shufer

They instinctively head for the sea.

When they reach maturity, they return to the same beach where they hatched to mate and lay eggs

For the next ten to twenty years, they swim in the ocean waters as they slowly mature.

Bayville Manor House

Bayville Manor was built in the early 19th century by Peter Singleton II on property that was part of the original Adam Thoroughgood grant. The privately owned house fronting Pleasure House Creek still stands on seven of the original acres contiguous to the Bayville Golf Club grounds on First Court Road. Look for the white frame manor house from Pleasure House Creek. As local residents have reported finding large numbers of artifacts such as arrowheads and pottery shards (Lester, 2002), we know that long before the white settlers arrived, this same area was frequented by Native Americans.

1953 Bayville Manor House - Eleanor Tyler Stanton, Stuart Baldwin, Calvert Tyler Lester

Courtesy of Calvert Lester

History of the Lynnhaven Oyster

"He is a bold man that first ate an oyster."
— Jonathan Swift (1667-1745)

Boldness not withstanding, it was the renowned Lynnhaven oyster that gave our waterways historical notoriety. The local shellfish was noted for its size and taste as far back as the 1600s. As history tells it, Captain George Percy and his eager explorers from England, during their second venture ashore in 1607, came across a fire where the native Chesapeake Indians had been roasting oysters. It is more than one historian's guess that this encounter with the smoking bivalves occurred at Little Neck Point. Much like Goldilocks who was tempted with abandoned bear porridge, the hungry Englishmen helped themselves to the Indian-prepared delicacy. Impressed taste buds prompted an entry in a journal, setting the reputation of the Lynnhaven oyster in motion.

The Lynnhaven oyster, extraordinarily nutritionally balanced for its appearance and texture, was quite popular by the 1800s (de Gast, 1970). While the Lynnhaven is the same species of oyster harvested all along the east coast of North America, the Lynnhaven River gained a reputation for having large, salty oysters because of its position near the bay's mouth.

Artwork by Kent Forrest, Courtesy of Virginia Institute Marine Science

Settlers enjoying oyster roast from which Indians had fled, 1607

The mollusks' size prompted the term "count" in oyster vocabulary, a name reserved for the Lynnhaven's huge bivalves: neither "standard" nor "select," the usual terms, did our oyster justice (Barrow, 1990). Ours could have been called "bigger than jumbo."

By the late 19th century, the Lynnhaven oyster had gained an international reputation and was a major export. President Taft's high praise for the delicacy in 1909, when he sampled it at O'Keefe's Oyster Pavilion at old Cape Henry, revitalized the oyster's reputation and popularity (Mansfield, 1989). In the season of 1929-30, almost 400,000 pounds of oysters were harvested from the leased oyster grounds in the Lynnhaven, but by 1931 small portions of the river were closed for direct market harvesting due to water contamination. Unfortunately, by the mid 1970s all shellfish harvesting in the Lynnhaven was off-limits. The dwindling supply of oysters was associated with over-harvesting, destruction of oyster reefs, contamination of the waters, and disease. Thankfully, with the work of several partner agencies and the cooperation of the public, the future is looking brighter for our native oyster. Water quality will surely improve as the native stocks of oysters become more plentiful. For information on how you can become an Oyster Gardener for the Chesapeake Bay Foundation, contact them at *www.cbf.org/oysters*.

John W. Keeling with enormous oyster

Courtesy of John W. Keeling

Paddlers' and Boaters' Note: The Lynnhaven is a shallow bay and it may be wise to follow channel markers or crab pot buoys at lower tide levels.

Morning Star Baptist Church

In the Bayville area is **Morning Star Baptist Church**. Organized in 1887 by members of the local Black community, this church was originally begun as a Sunday school for youngsters whose parents were concerned by what was a rather long walk to the nearest existing church. The Sunday morning meetings soon attracted larger numbers of people and prayer services were added for the adults. As with most early church groups, these meetings and the Sunday school classes were held at someone's home. After two years, the congregation was able to erect a church building on what was then the Garrison Plantation. During the early years, two local pastors, Reverend Elisha White and Reverend Charlie Logan, offered to serve the congregation as time permitted. The congregation was also led by two ministers who preached sermons when they could, and was eventually served by a minister from Norfolk, the Reverend Madison Louis, who visited once a month to offer communion.

On February 3, 1892, Lansing D. Wetmore, the owner in residence of nearby Bayville Manor, sold the trustees of Morning Star Baptist Church the land for the sum of one

Artwork by Lu Hou, Courtesy of City of Virginia Beach, VA

dollar (Hawkins-Hendrix, 1998). Currently there is more than one structure on the original plot of land, but the original building still stands. Not visible today, it is intact beneath the current brickwork, completed in 1972 at 4800 First Court Road, Virginia Beach, VA 23455. For more information, call (757) 464-3663.

Destination 2: *Church Point*

Paddling or boating southwest from Pleasure House Creek, one will pass **Church Point**, named for the first colonial church built in 1639 by Adam Thoroughgood. By 1691, the church was abandoned because it had become "ruinous" and the river was claiming its grounds. A new place of worship was under construction. According to a church order of 1689, this new structure made of brick was to be completed by the end of June, 1692 (Mason, 1949). By 1733 orders for another church were issued as the first brick church proved too small for the growing population. It was occupied by 1736 and part of it is the present Old Donation Episcopal Church.

Church Point is also the site of one of the first courthouses for Princess Anne County. Read about the history of the courthouses on page 44.

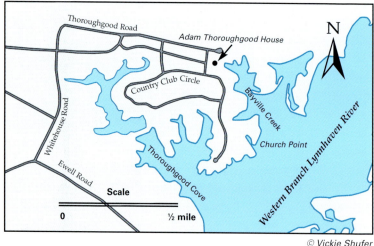

© *Vickie Shufer*

Church Point, 1639 - Memorial presented by Suffolk Chapter Virginia Society National Society Colonial Dames XVII Century 1995

The Lynnhaven River yields some of its treasures. Taken from the waters near the site of the first parish church was a red marble baptismal font, apparently used ignobly as a makeshift anchor when found (Nash, 2000). The font, dating back to the 1600s, was even in the 1800s one of the few remaining "venerable relics of antiquity" donated in colonial days to the Episcopal Church (Walke, circa 1890). Of this same sacred ornament, Henry Walke of the Walke family associated with Ferry Plantation wrote in his memoirs over a century ago, "hundreds of the good people of the county have stood before its ample basin to receive the holy sacrament of baptism." To this day, the baptismal font withstands the test of time within Old Donation Church as it continues to serve at every baptism.

Photo by Lillie Gilbert

History of the Courthouses

The area that is today Virginia Beach was originally part of the Elizabeth City Shire during colonial days. This shire in 1634 included land on both sides of Hampton Roads and contained fewer than 2,000 people. By 1637 the land of the Elizabeth City Shire (County) that was south of Hampton Roads was then named New Norfolk County. The next year, New Norfolk was split into Upper and Lower Norfolk County.

In 1661 the first courthouse in Lower Norfolk was built on Broad Creek. Two courthouses replaced this one in 1689, again close to water. They were situated on the Elizabeth River and Wolfsnare Creek (off the Eastern Branch of the Lynnhaven River). In 1691, the House of Burgesses formed the new county of Princess Anne from the eastern part of Lower Norfolk County. In 1695 the Wolfsnare courthouse was broken down and its parts timbers relocated to the west side of the Lynnhaven River next to where Old Donation Church now stands. Four more moves were in store, the first in 1735 to a ferry landing close by on the Lynnhaven, very near the William Walke Manor House that preceded the Ferry Plantation House. The courthouse, built at the ferry landing, was the first in Princess Anne County to be made of brick. The courthouse property contained a stock and pillory located outdoors where those accused of various crimes, including minor offenses, were displayed for public ridicule. The next courthouse was at the busy port village of New Town (today's Newtown Road area) from 1752-1778. From New Town, the courthouse next moved in 1778 to Kempe's Landing, then a commercial port with several stores, riverfront warehouses and at least one public house that offered dining. Kempe's Landing incorporated into the town of Kempsville in 1783.

The final courthouse move occurred in 1824 when the county's court was seated at the current location on Princess Anne Road, representing a more geographic center. The court's location had followed population shifts and by 1800, the population of Princess Anne County was comprised of over 8,800 souls (Mansfield, 1989).

Leaping ahead 200 years to the twenty-first century, the city of Virginia Beach is involved in e-government with the website at *www.VBgov.com*. A list of canoe and kayak access sites is on the Parks and Recreation link of the city's website.

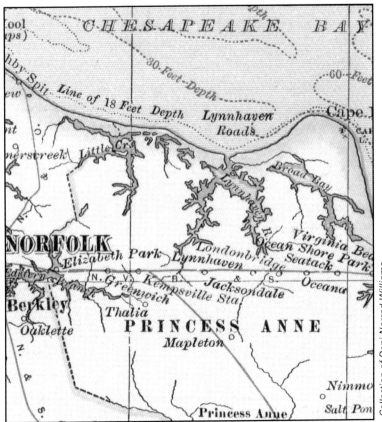

The Century Atlas, Virginia, 1897

> *When we see the land as a community to which we belong, we may begin to use it with love and respect.*
> – Aldo Leopold

Towns on the Rivers

The British authorities repeatedly sought to legislate riverside towns into being in the Virginia colony, primarily to serve as central points for trading. It was the Crown's goal to circumvent the costs and frustrations of sending English ships to privately owned plantation wharves for imports and exports. Apparently, captains of these ships were disgruntled about sailing in the sometimes mosquito-prone, unfamiliar shallows of the backwaters, and using their own men to load the heavy hogsheads of tobacco (Tazewell & Friddell, 2000).

The Assembly of March, 1654/5 passed a law entitled "An Act for Regulating Trade and Establishing Ports and Places for Markets." The act specified that ports and market places be established "in each parish on a river," and that within these sites should be located the County Court, the clerk's office, the Sheriff's office and the prison. The act was repealed in 1656 and the court, so it seems, rotated between Lynnhaven and Elizabeth Rivers for the next several years, more times than not in the homes of the vestrymen (Whichard, 1959).

In 1679, the Crown again instructed the governor of Virginia "'to endeavor all you can to dispose the planters to build towns upon every river, and especially one at least on every great river, as tending very much to their security and profit." Objections of the merchants led to the suspension of this proposed system. The idea of towns was not rejected, but these later cropped up when colonists were settling away from the water's edge (Tazewell & Friddell, 2000).

Natural history, then, provides the thread on which cultural history grips and forms itself.

– Dr. Mark Sagoff

For cigarettes, Virginia tobacco is the best.

Ad from **The Princess Anne Times**, *1917*

Little Neck

Across from Church Point is **Little Neck**, the area that served as glebe land for the church. "Glebes" were the lands belonging to the church, often granted by the King or donated by the more affluent church members. Revenue from farming the glebes, by and large the cash crop tobacco, was used to pay the clergy. It is believed the minister's home was at the northern tip of the peninsula, the area marked by large, old trees. The northernmost tip of Little Neck was long ago referred to as Trading Point, as seen on various maps of earlier days. Today, this "glebe land" encompasses the modern subdivisions of Middle Plantation, Sea Breeze Farms, and King's Grant (Clark, 1991). Many coves to the east allow the paddler ample opportunities for exploration.

In the 1735 court records of early Princess Anne County, it is written that a log bridge was being built to cross the Lynnhaven, a much narrower river then, somewhere between Thoroughgood's land on the northern shore of Ferry Point and Little Neck, now called King's Grant (White, 1924). There is a 1909 photograph of a Barnett family oyster roast that clearly shows the remains of bridge pilings extending all the way across this part of the river. The Barnett family owned Ferry Plantation House from circa 1898 to the 1940s.

Photo from the collection of Ann Parks Courtesy of Ferry Plantation House

Old Cypress Bridge Post - There are today remains of what appear to be the corduroy road log placement that would provide the entrance to what was probably the log bridge. Look for these and at least three old wooden posts along the shore of the Lynnhaven near Ferry Plantation; there are as many on the opposite shore.

Photo by Belinda Nash

It is also at Little Neck that the *S. G. Keeling Oyster Roast* restaurant, one of several oyster houses on this peninsula in past days, operated riverside at the north end of West Little Neck Road. Its heyday of serving a local mollusk-loving clientele was in the 1920s through the 1940s. Before shellfishing was banned, Solomon Godfrey Keeling (1881-1967), followed by his son, John Wesley Keeling, with lineage going back to early settler and waterman Adam Keeling, leased about 100 acres of oyster beds from the state. Keeling's Oyster Cove is still marked on some maps of the river. The family business supplied their own and other local restaurants with a succulent harvest. The Keeling ad ran as follows:

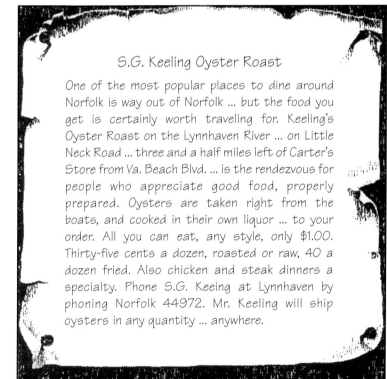

S.G. Keeling Oyster Roast

One of the most popular places to dine around Norfolk is way out of Norfolk ... but the food you get is certainly worth traveling for. Keeling's Oyster Roast on the Lynnhaven River ... on Little Neck Road ... three and a half miles left of Carter's Store from Va. Beach Blvd. ... is the rendezvous for people who appreciate good food, properly prepared. Oysters are taken right from the boats, and cooked in their own liquor ... to your order. All you can eat, any style, only $1.00. Thirty-five cents a dozen, roasted or raw, 40 a dozen fried. Also chicken and steak dinners a specialty. Phone S.G. Keeing at Lynnhaven by phoning Norfolk 44972. Mr. Keeling will ship oysters in any quantity ... anywhere.

Courtesy of John W. Keeling

Destination 3: *Thoroughgood Cove*

The next cove to the south of Church Point is **Thoroughgood Cove**, named for Captain Adam Thoroughgood, who received a land grant for 5,350 acres on 24 June 1635 (Nugent, 1992). The English cottage home, which now bears his name, was built circa 1680 by one of his descendants and is open to the public for guided tours. Call (757) 460-7588. This oldest brick home in the US is located at 1636 Parish Road in Virginia Beach, VA 23455. The house is open for visitation year-round, but is closed on Mondays.

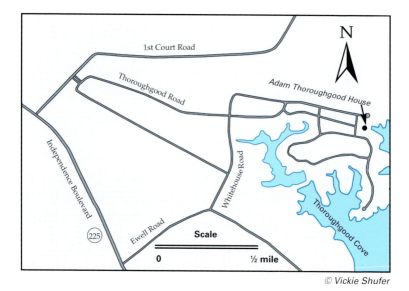

© Vickie Shufer

Adam Thoroughgood

Adam Thoroughgood came to the colonies from England as an educated and religious young man. Being the seventh son of an English vicar, however, Adam had no money in his pockets and few prospects. He arrived in Virginia as an indentured servant. When his term was completed, he returned to England and married Sarah Offley (1609-1657) of a wealthy London family. He then returned to Virginia with hopes of colonizing (Turner, 1984).

Thoroughgood originally settled in Kicotan (Kecoughtan), Virginia, today's nearby city of Hampton. It was not until 1634, over a decade after the first party from England landed at Cape Henry, that he moved to Lynnhaven Bay as one of the first settlers of our area. An ambitious man, he quickly became an established leader. Early records show him as an elected member of the House of Burgesses and the Governor's Council. He was appointed Commissioner (Justice) and later Commander (Presiding Justice) of the county.

Church vestry books indicate that it was Thoroughgood who generously donated land for the first church of Lynnhaven Parish, which was built in 1639 at Church Point. He also drew up the boundaries for Lynnhaven Parish, which later became the boundaries of Princess Anne County and then later almost exactly the boundaries of Virginia Beach.

In anticipation of a large patent coming his way for his part in bringing 105 persons to the colony (using his wife's dowry, it seems), Adam Thoroughgood surveyed the lands of

Adam Thoroughgood House

his choice and, in 1635, applied for an extremely large land grant. The industrious colonist was granted over 5,000 acres and ultimately came to own about 7,000 acres of land, most of what is today's Bayside.

Adam Thoroughgood died in 1640, well accomplished for one in his mid 30s. The original Thoroughgood manor house and plantation in the vicinity of today's Thoroughgood neighborhood was bequeathed to his wife Sarah. Son Adam inherited the remaining lands and houses. The house that stands today (built by a descendant) passed through many owners and was purchased by the Adam Thoroughgood Foundation in 1957 when restoration began. It was given to the City of Norfolk by the Foundation on March 21, 1961 (Norfolk Museum Bulletin, 1961). The ownership at the time of this publication is through the City of Norfolk although the property is managed by the City of Virginia Beach.

John Gookin's Landing

John Gookin's Landing place "on the Wigtown shore of the Linhaven River" was located towards the head of Samuell Bennetts Creek, which is now the Thurston Branch (Nugent, 1992). Based on its relative position to neighboring tracts of land as stated in deeds, the landing was probably on one or the other side of Thoroughgood Cove. Captain John Gookin (circa 1613-1643) was the son of Daniel Gookin, a wealthy landowner from Ireland who had settled in Newport News in the 1620s. In 1641, John received a grant of 640 acres of land on Samuell Bennetts Creek adjoining Adam Thoroughgood's tract. He relocated there from Nansemond County (now Suffolk) northwest across the bay and soon became the second husband to Adam Thoroughgood's widow Sarah. In marrying Sarah, Gookin fell heir not only to Thoroughgood's lands but also to the deceased man's positions in the community, becoming a Captain, then a Colonel in the militia, a vestryman of the church, and a Justice of the county (Turner, 1984).

There are historical references to a tavern near the mouth of the Lynnhaven River kept by Mrs. Sarah Gookin (White, 1924). If located at her second husband's John Gookin's Landing, most likely it was near the first courthouse. Taverns of the day were customarily located near the courthouses with the intention of serving those in attendance, many of whom wished to imbibe and socialize between and after sessions and some of whom needed to stay overnight due to the long return distances to their homes (Turner, 1984). In fact, in 1654 an act of the Crown charged Justices to "endeavor to have meeting places or churches and ordinaries for entertainment and lodging within the same" (Whichard, 1959).

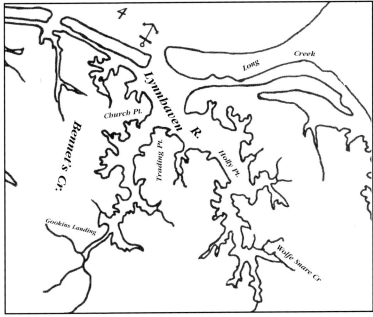

Old Map Courtesy of Norfolk Public Library

> *In some counties bordering on the Chesapeake Bay, nearly every other man resident, whether he be the owner of a "dugout" ... or the master of a coasting schooner, has the title of "Captain."*
> – James McDonald

Destination 4: *Witch Duck Bay*

The next series of coves to the south are named **Witch Duck Bay**. The name comes from the court case of Grace Sherwood who consented to a trial by ducking in July of 1706 to see if she was indeed a witch, as several of her neighbors believed.

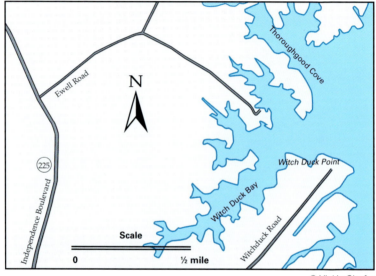

© Vickie Shufer

In addition to the site of the famous trial, there was a windmill near Witch Duck Point that was in use during colonial times. It was part of the William Walke property settled in the 1730s. The remains of the trough dug for retention of the tidal waters for the "tidal windmill" are visible today and located on private property on the bay front (*Ferry Tidings*, 1998). This was one of two windmills on the Western Branch of the Lynnhaven for which one of these authors has found documentation. In colonial times, windmills were set up for private use and could be utilized by the general community upon payment of a percentage of the product. Mills were used for grinding or providing power for sawing lumber. This one was most likely used for grains and corn.

Artwork by Casey Holtzinger, Courtesy of Imperial Gallery and Frame Shop

Grace Sherwood

One of the most famous residents of the region was Grace Sherwood, who with her husband, farmed land near Muddy Creek in the Pungo area of Princess Anne County, VA. She is remembered as "The Witch of Pungo." Known locally as a healer, possessing knowledge of herbs, and generally being a non-conformist, Grace was sued and she counter-sued a number of times over a nine-year period prior to her punishment date of July 10, 1706. As was the custom, the Sherwoods had to pay all court costs as well as room and board for her family and all witnesses related to the case.

Courtesy of the artist, William Rylance

Finally after a trial for witchcraft, the only trial by water in the history of Virginia, Grace was found guilty after being ducked in the Lynnhaven River near a place now called "Witch Duck Point." The sheriff's posse with Grace was in

Witch Ducking in 1706, Grace Sherwood *Courtesy of the artist, Charles Sibley*

one boat and the jury in another. Both boats were rowed 200 yards off shore. She was tied crossbound, the manner known customary for ducking, with her right thumb to her left toe and her left thumb to her right toe. Ropes were tied to her with each boat having a lead, as instructed by the vicar so that if she sank she could be hauled out at the last moment. This great care being taken, she was cast into the river. Grace did float rather than sink. Ironically, had she sunk, this would have proven her innocence. She was given a seven-year sentence and was imprisoned. After her incarceration, on 16 June 1714, Grace reacquired 145 acres of land in exchange for "2 lbs. Tobacco, &c." (Nugent, 1992). She was the only woman in Princess Anne County to be granted land by the capital at Williamsburg during 1714. This is part of the original land (50 acres) given to Grace and her husband, James, as a wedding present by her father, John White, in 1680. After the death of her father the following year, Grace inherited most of the balance of land he formerly owned, an original total of 195 acres. Apparently, in order to reclaim her land after her incarceration she had to pay the back taxes. What happened to the other 50 acres is open to speculation. As Grace had many court costs to pay, it may be that part of her land was taken as payment.

Grace's land at Muddy Creek was bordered by a pocosin and Asheville Creek (now called Asheville Bridge Creek). Muddy Creek and Muddy Creek Road are still so-named as are Witch Duck Point and Witch Duck Bay on the western side of the Lynnhaven River, the site of her ducking. She died in 1740 at age 80 leaving the 145 acres to her eldest son and to her other two heirs a small legacy. Grace Sherwood is still the subject of local folklore as "The Witch of Pungo," made famous in a book of the same name by the late beloved local author, Louisa Venable Kyle (1903-1999).

Kayaking Into History

July 10, 2002 marked the first tracing by water to the exact spot where Grace Sherwood was ducked, its location having been researched by Belinda Nash. For the event, the site had been marked with a PVC post out in the water by some of Belinda's friends. She then sponsored a kayak trip to be at the site at the precise time of day when the ducking took place, 296 years before.

Belinda has spent over 18 years researching the life of Grace Sherwood. In period costume, she interprets Grace's life at the historic Ferry Plantation House and to various civic

Belinda Nash and Gerry Richtech at the Ducking Site   *Photo by Lillie Gilbert*

groups and organizations. To hear her account of the kayaking experience is chilling:

> *For many years I had rung the bell at Old Donation Church at '10 of ye clock' as the court record states was the time that Grace was taken from the courthouse down the dirt path, approximately one mile to the ducking point. This anniversary trip by water from Ferry Plantation House was approximately a one and a half mile paddle by kayak.*
>
> *Upon arriving at the pre-marked spot and gazing at the shore where Grace herself had once had the same water view, the adrenaline flow was incredible. I pictured the hundreds of people lining the shore chanting, 'Duck the Witch, Duck the Witch.' As I have devoted so many years of research to fully understand what Grace Sherwood had gone through, this was the most incredible experience for me.*

The Chapel at Haygood United Methodist Church

This chapel, originally a church, is brought to the reader's attention as it is listed along the Bayside History Trail by land. It is not visible from the water and is the most distant structure from the Lynnhaven River of those discussed in this book. We are including it because of its significance to the communities that were served by it. This small attractive church, built in 1896, was originally called Haygood Methodist Memorial in honor of Bishop Atticus G. Haygood. Serving as a sanctuary until 1968 when the new church was constructed, this structure was built on the site of the 1832 Ebenezer Methodist Episcopal Church South. Wood recovered from the first church was used to construct the chapel's pulpit. In the chapel are displayed a Bible from the 1850s and

Haygood Chapel   Photo by Deni Norred-Williams

an antique organ. Services are held in the chapel every Sunday at 8:30 AM and Wednesday nights at 7 PM. The chapel is located at 4713 Haygood Road, Virginia Beach, VA 23455. The phone number is (757) 499-1269.

Lynnhaven House

Erroneously known for a long time as the Wishart House, this small, soundly constructed brick house, circa 1725, sits on five acres in a serene, country-like setting near the Lynnhaven River. Built seven years before George Washington was born, this house is considered to be one of the best preserved of the early dwellings in the United States. While the house stands on what historians say was the land of 17th century ferry operator Savill Gaskin, it was built much later, probably by Francis Thelaball, who bought the 250 acres of property in 1721 (Turner, 1984). Ownership later went to the affluent Boush family, and there are four of their gravestones remaining in the cemetery on the grounds.

Courtesy of the artist, William Rylance

Fashioned transitionally in architecture, the story and a half house features large north and south step chimneys and Georgian dormer windows. The house includes two rooms downstairs, a kitchen and "the Hall." A stairway rising from the back of this hall leads to two upstairs bedrooms, and an attic storeroom located under the steep roof. In the cellar with its great wood beams were found, said Turner, "evidences of casks of sack [an imported Spanish wine] and brandy." The Lynnhaven House is owned and restored by *The Association for the Preservation of Virginia Antiquities*, having been bequeathed by the Oliver family in 1971. After meticulous restoration and preservation, it was opened to the public in 1976. The house may be visited at 4405 Wishart Road, Virginia Beach, VA 23455. For more information, call (757) 460-1688.

> *To live by a large river is to be kept in the heart of things.*
> – John Haines

Old Donation Episcopal Church

The first church services ever held in Lynnhaven Parish were in 1637 at the home of Adam Thoroughgood. This marked the establishment of the Old Donation Church as it was the third in a continuum of the Lynnhaven Parish Churches. As early as 1639, the first Lynnhaven Parish Church was built on land donated by Mr. Thoroughgood. As that building deteriorated and became unusable, in 1691 the vestry of the church called for another building to be constructed. This was accomplished by 1692. As the membership grew, a new, larger church needed to be built and this church, completed in 1736, is what we now are able to visit (in reconstructed form) on the Bayside History Trail by land.

Courtesy of the artist, William Rylance

The church got its name from the property left to it in the will of the Reverend Robert Dickson in 1776. The land was to be used as a school and the area became known as "Donation Farm." The church in close proximity became known as Old Donation Church.

Church Ruins, 1900   *Photo from collection of Ferry Plantation House*

This old church suffered the growing pains and transitory nature of an increasing population. Other churches and chapels were built and by 1842, Old Donation was abandoned. By 1882 it had burned with only parts of walls left standing. Loyal churchgoers still held services in the ruins at least once a year so that by law the church would not revert to state property (Kyle, 1969). In 1912 reconstruction began due to the efforts of a dedicated group of supporters led in part by the Reverend Richard Alfriend and Judge Benjamin Dey White. Old Donation was rebuilt by 1916 and its bell tower by 1923. Still in use are the colonial silver communion goblet and flagon, dated 1712 and 1716, respectively, given to the first brick church by Princess Anne, later, Queen Anne (*The Beach*, 1996). By the 1960s structural repairs were needed, and the slate floors were added. All work was completed by 1966.

In 1997, underwater archaeologists tentatively located areas where the remains of the first Lynnhaven Parish Church and cemetery lay buried in the sand and silt at Church Point. Brett Phaneuf of Marine Sonics Technology and John Broadwater, underwater archaeologist, manager of the Monitor National Marine Sanctuary, and overseer of the successful and historic Monitor Project (sponsored in part by the Commerce Department's National Oceanic and

Atmospheric Administration) headquartered at The Mariners' Museum in Newport News, VA, led the exploration on the Lynnhaven River. In less than an hour the hunt showed rectangular objects that may be headstones as well as some structural debris that could possibly be the church foundation. It is hoped that further investigation will prove what has long been believed by locals: the foundation of the 17th century Lynnhaven Parish Church and its graveyard are at the bottom of the Lynnhaven River off Church Point. The Lynnhaven keeps its secrets well hidden today, but it is said that tombstones were visible through the water as recently as 100 years ago (Barrow, 1997).

Outdoor Church Service held in ruins, 1901   *Photo from collection of Edgar Brown*

Courtesy of the artist, William Rylance

Ferry Plantation House

Standing just slightly inland on a lovely point on the Western Branch of the Lynnhaven River is **Ferry Plantation House**. Located at 4136 Cheswick Lane, Virginia Beach, VA 23455, this ten-room Federal farmhouse with a central passage plan features three-course American bond brickwork, interior shutters, country Greek Revival mantels, six-inch heart pine flooring, and horse hair plaster. The farmhouse that stands today was built by George McIntosh for his son Charles McIntosh around 1830 from the good brick of the original **Walke Manor House** that was destroyed by fire.

The first recorded reference to the property is a 1642 court record regarding the ferry service. Ferry Plantation is also the location of the third Princess Anne`County courthouse, which then included stocks and pillory. The Anthony Walke tavern site was, in 1986, the largest artifact find in Virginia. The fifty thousand artifacts uncovered by Robert R. Hunter Jr., an archaeologist from Colonial Williamsburg Foundation, are now stored in Williamsburg, VA (Fairlamb et al., 1996).

From the water, look for the one-lane concrete boat ramp which is closed by a metal gate. It will be on the southeast end of a peninsula of land where the Western Branch of the Lynnhaven River, Thurston Branch and Buchannan Creek intersect. See map on page 69. This is a private community boat ramp, so do not use it without permission of the landowners. Do take a moment to look past the new homes at the waterfront and about 50 yards from the water's edge behind the boat ramp, where Ferry Plantation House can still be seen. Imagine this view without the neighboring homes when the entire area was farmed and the boat ramp was the actual ferry landing.

The Ferry Plantation House is open to the public on Tuesdays and Thursdays and is being preserved/renovated for adaptive reuse as an historic site and research center. Call (757) 473-5626 for information on tours.

1 - Old Ferry Landing; 2 - Site of Log Bridge; 3 - Ferry Plantation House

Photo from Collection of Belinda Nash, Courtesy of John Blow

The Lynnhaven Ferry System

The ferryboat is part of our proud waterborne heritage. Ferries were one of the first public services of the colonies. In fact, the Court established early on that ferries were a public responsibility and should be supported by public levy (Whichard, 1959). A 1642 court record introduces the colorful character, Savill Gaskin, Lynnhaven River's ferry operator. The Frenchman, a former indentured servant whom court records say habitually stayed in debt, lived on the lands where the **Lynnhaven House** is now located. His tract of land was known as Scull Neck (Turner, 1984).

A rendering of the 1636 Elizabeth River Ferry, first established by Adam Thoroughgood. This skiff was rowed and carried foot passengers across the river.

On a ferry not much bigger than a very large rowboat, Gaskin brought passengers to and from various destinations or points along the river and its tributaries. Local lore says one ferry stop, Two Penny Point, was named such for the price of riding the ferry or for ferrying from one to another point. The ferry could hold several passengers, their goods, and even a horse. As ferry service was a main source of travel, it allowed foot travelers of the area, with no other means of transportation, to reach their destinations.

There was no regular ferry schedule. To summon the ferry operator, passengers waiting may have fired a signal cannon. These small cannons are thought to have been placed at every point along the rivulet. The ferry operator would heed the signal call "upon notice by a hollow [holler?] or a ffeir [firing of a cannon?]" (Whichard, 1959). According to oral accounts of residents, three of these signal cannons have been found in the **Ferry Plantation** area. Two were reportedly taken from the water over thirty years ago, but one has since "disappeared" and the second crumbled as it was removed from its watery grave. The third is said to still rest in the salt water off the point that she signaled.

White Acres

Just to the northwest of Witch Duck Bay and Witch Duck Point, in the vicinity of today's Independence Middle School, was the birthplace and childhood home of the esteemed Judge Benjamin Dey White (1868-1946). In 1911, he acquired ownership of his ancestral 167-acre Bayside farm. After developing its grounds, **White Acres** was considered one of the show places of the county. An avid reader, Judge White was especially interested in matters of wildlife conservation and horticulture. In keeping with his love of fauna and flora, peacocks, geese, dogs, and wild fowl roamed the grounds of his Bayside estate (Tazewell, 1991).

Judge White lived in Princess Anne County most of his life. He served as judge of the 28th Judicial Circuit Court and presided over the circuit's four counties for 38 years. He was known by his fellow jurists for his "speedy administration of justice," and was said to preside "with distinction and dispatch" (*The Virginian-Pilot*, 1946).

Collection of Belinda Nash

In addition to such devout attention to his duties, Judge White was considered one of the best authorities of his times on the history of Princess Anne County; he authored many "sketches" of the county's history and progress He kept a large collection of photographs of the area, which have been shared with others. Dedicated to the preservation of the county's history, he was instrumental in the rebuilding of Old Donation Church, finished in 1916.

Collection of Belinda Nash

> **Paddlers' and Boaters' Note:** Back to the Lynnhaven River, the paddler or boater, still traveling south, is now only 2 miles from the starting point at Crab Creek, but the distance may be a lot more if exploring in smaller coves. Motorized craft may find the water too shallow outside of the dredge channels. A map or compass might be useful since it is so easy to get disoriented.
>
> On the east shore the boater or paddler will pass **Hebden Cove** of the Little Neck peninsula. It is so-named after the Hebden family, inhabitants of the Little Neck area from at least the 1800s. If time permits, explore the coves of the eastern side of this Western Branch of the Lynnhaven River. Imagine the wooded areas as hunting grounds of the Native Americans, or the gentle slopes to the water as landings utilized by the early settlers as a means to get crops to the waiting cargo boats.

> *The rivers are our brothers. They quench our thirst. They carry our canoes and feed our children. You must give to the rivers the kindness you would give to any brother.*
>
> Chief Seattle

Destination 5: Thurston Branch

Continuing south past Witch Duck Bay, the river splits into two smaller branches: **Thurston Branch** to the west and **Buchannan Creek** to the east. Most paddlers call it quits here and retrace the route back to Crab Creek. Motor boaters will need to be aware of shallow water on either side of the dredged channel. Heading west is a small creek with an historic past. Thurston Branch was earlier called Bennetts Creek and tracing the origin of its name has proved interesting.

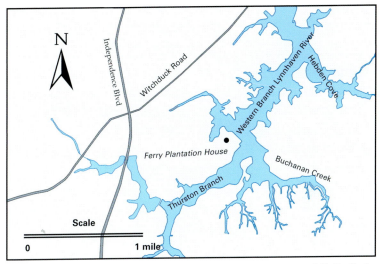

© Vickie Shufer

History of Thurston Branch/Bennetts Creek

At least as early as 1637 Thalia Creek or, depending upon the map, the entire Thurston Branch of the Lynnhaven River, was referred to as *Samuell Bennetts Creek*, sometimes just as *Bennetts Creek*. For whom was this waterway named? Early records' references to three different creeks of the same name befuddles the issue: in addition to this *Bennetts Creek* of Lynnhaven River long ago, there is another in Poquoson of York County and a third in what was then Nansemond County and now is the city of Suffolk. Scouring abstracted

> **Paddlers' Note:** If planning to paddle all the way to Mount Trashmore, check the tide and pick a high water day, as the creek gets very shallow and narrow. A trip under the interstate highway may prove to be impassable.

land patents for references to both Samuell Bennett the colonist and the tributary of his name yields no perfect match of person and place. However, the tidbits that did turn up contributed to one of this book's author's culminating theory, which is as follows.

The earliest reference found to the creek's probable namesake is in the year 1622, when a Samuell Bennett (1584/5- circa 1636) and his wife Joane are listed as servants to master William Tiler, an inhabitant of Virginia's "Elzabeth Cittie beyond Hampton River." Bennett, age 40, and his wife had come to Virginia that year on the *Providence* (Meyer & Dorman, 1987).

In 1633, a Samuell Bennett (for lack of others of this time period, more than likely the same one) is listed in a patent as having tenure of 50 acres in Elizabeth "Citty" (Nugent, 1992). Lynnhaven River's Thurston Branch may have been named after this Samuell. Old Elizabeth City, one of the eight original shires of Virginia created in 1634, was quite extensive in its territory. The boundaries of the shire then encompassed the Lynnhaven River, including the tributary in question. Conceivably, and in the tradition of Adam Thoroughgood, it may be that Bennett completed his indenture of slavery and purchased his own land when a free man. More than likely the contemporaneous Samuell Bennett and Adam Thoroughgood were acquaintances.

Other patents of the mid to late 1630s (Nugent, 1992) refer to "Samuell Bennetts Plantation" in the New Poquoson parish of what was then Charles River (now York) County, another of the original eight shires. It is hypothesized that this is one and the same Samuell Bennett, the gentleman having settled north of his earlier claim and holding the honor of yet another creek named after him … unless, of course, he named the creeks himself … and if so, more power to him. Samuell Bennett's wife, then later his daughter became heir of his plantation on the peninsula.

Bennetts Creek remains today the name of a stream in the city of Poquoson. Likewise, a populated area and river in Suffolk continues to go by the name. Lynnhaven River's *Bennetts Creek*, however, has long since been renamed as **Thurston Branch.**

Destination 6: *Thalia Creek*

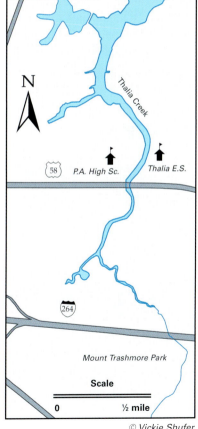

Thurston Branch ends at **Thalia Creek**, which eventually winds its way to **Mount Trashmore Park's Lake Windsor.** The total distance by water from Thalia Creek to Lake Windsor is 2.2 miles. At low water, the paddler might want to turn around at Virginia Beach Boulevard, making the distance on Thalia Creek only one mile from its confluence with Thurston Branch.

This area is heavily populated, but still nice paddling. Traveling along Thalia Creek, the boater will pass Thalia Elementary School on the east side of the creek and Princess Anne High School on the

© Vickie Shufer

west. It is in this vicinity that the **McIntosh Bridge**, named after Thalia's Summerville Plantation's Scottish proprietor, once connected the creek's opposing banks. The crossings of it today are at US 58/Virginia Beach Boulevard, the railroad bridge, Bonney Road, and the culvert for Interstate 264. Future plans call for a greenway/blueway network to connect this waterway with The Town Center complex across from Pembroke Mall. It is from Thalia Creek that the paddler sees the tall tower of The Town Center complex.

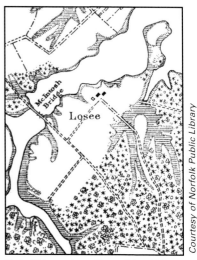
Part of Princess Anne County Map, 1881
Courtesy of Norfolk Public Library

Railroad bridge across Thalia Creek, looking south

Photo by Deni Norred-Williams

A fine waterfront restaurant along this route is **Steinhilber's Thalia Acres Inn** located at 653 Thalia Road (by land). Locals rave about Steinhilber's fried shrimp as being the finest anywhere. Call first for a reservation if you

have a party of 8 or more, (757) 340-1156, and if you decide to arrive by boat, inquire about taking out on the property. There is plenty of parking. Ask about proper attire if staying for dinner. Remember to bring a change of clothes and to plan a shuttle vehicle to return you to your put-in location.

Lynnhaven Golf and Country Club, 1920s

History of Thalia

Steinhilbers, a dining tradition since 1939, was built on the burnt foundation of the old clubhouse of the **Lynnhaven Golf and Country Club**, which served the area's Jewish elite during the Roaring Twenties. Before Robert Steinhilber built the restaurant he offered horseback riding and canoeing at this waterfront site.

Steinhilbers, view from the water with magnolia tree   *Photo by Lillie Gilbert*

Today's canoeist or kayaker, with a glance to the southeast bank, will see a view of a magnificent magnolia tree on the restaurant's back lawn. This survivor of the country club days bears a scar from the fire that local legend says accounted for the club's demise (Flachsenhaar, 1995).

Even further back in time, the 19th century white stucco, flat-topped **Summerville Plantation** Manor House overlooked the river from the same vicinity. Boaters of those days could spy the plantation's lofty windmill on the banks as they neared the plantation from the river (Walke, circa 1890).

That George McIntosh of Summerville Plantation married Elizabeth Walke of **Ferry Plantation,** up and across the river (north and west of Summerville), bears testimony to the frequent occurrence of earlier Princess Anne County families connected by marriage. Said Louisa Venable Kyle (1956) of this phenomenon and the river, "There was much water traffic in those days when barges and sailing skiffs carried these cousins, for sooner or later most of these families were related by marriage, moving back and forth across the river as they did for visits ... and parties."

Summerville Plantation Manor House   Artwork © 2003, Scott Denham

Continuing on the creek as it is today, before it meanders under Virginia Beach Boulevard and not too far from the water is the former location of **Camp Ashby**, a Prisoner of War (POW) camp during World War II. The POW camp was completely demolished after the war except for a few buildings that were converted to residences. These are inconspicuously scattered in the Thalia Manor neighborhood. Read about this POW Camp on page 78.

Thalia Creek connects to Lake Windsor at Mount Trashmore. Because of the connection with Thalia to the Lynnhaven, these waters are brackish and support finfish and the occasional marine species. The vegetated shoreline of Thalia Creek consists mostly of phragmites, but there are patches of non-invasive marsh grasses as well. The native habitat supports wading birds and various seasonal waterfowl. The latest dredging of the Western Branch and the smaller creeks began in 1998 with all work being completed in 2000. Because of the water quality, shellfish that are native to this creek are not to be eaten. The end of the dredged channel is near Thalia Elementary School and is marked by a sign. Travel by canoe or kayak further upstream should be attempted only at high tide.

Deni Norred-Williams paddling Thalia Creek   *Photo by Lillie Gilbert*

History of Timber Necke and Pembroke

In the colonial period, a tract of land south of Pembroke on the west bank, then called **Timber Necke** (now, Princess Anne High School, Pembroke Mall and Pembroke East Shoppes), was part of Adam Thoroughgood's landholdings. Timber Necke was later "taken up by" the colonial planter Colonel Francis Yeardley (1624-1655), son of Sir George Yeardley, who twice served as Governor of Virginia during the colonial period (Fleet, 1988). As an aside, Yeardley became Sarah Offley Thoroughgood Gookin's third husband. Nearly a century later, other local historical figures owning Timber Necke included John Ellegood and Captain John Saunders (McIntosh, 1924). The latter colonial planter was associated

Artwork by Casey Holtzinger, Courtesy of Imperial Gallery and Frame Shop

with the **Pembroke Manor House**, which was later a dairy farmhouse and today serves as the Ivy League Academy Christian Learning Center on the former Pembroke Plantation north of and across the creek from Thalia. The address is 520 Constitution Drive, Virginia Beach, VA 23462. For information, call (757) 499-6064.

Pembroke Manor House as it appears today

German Prisoner of War Camp

Near Thalia Creek, part of the current Willis Furniture complex is the former tuberculosis hospital, Tidewater Victory Memorial Hospital, completed in the winter of 1937. In 1941 the Army leased the hospital from the state of Virginia and built Camp Thalia as an army barracks on grounds surrounding the hospital. The defunct hospital became the administrative center for the camp. Early into World War II, the compound was renamed Camp Ashby and it was quickly converted to a POW camp. The camp housed a total of 6,000 German prisoners of war during its operation from 1944-1946 with a peak capacity of 1,788 one year. Only those prisoners with anti-Nazi sentiments were allowed on the Tidewater work details. Others were sent to a camp in Arizona.

Since so much of the work force of Tidewater was absent from the area during the war, the prisoners were looked upon as a vital labor source. They planted and picked vegetables, worked on local dairy farms, dug ditches around the area, and worked as laborers at Fort Story. Workers were given a stipend as wages and the amount remaining after most was placed in a savings account could be spent for movies shown at the camp or for articles at the camp store. One of the former POWs visited Virginia Beach in 1985 and remarked that he had been treated and fed very well and was surprised to be given $98 when the camp closed in March 1946. The camp allowed the Germans to produce their own newspaper featuring world and local news as well as puzzles and English lessons (Barrow, 1985). After the war, Willis Furniture Company purchased the administration building in 1950 (Mansfield, 1989).

Afterword

We hope you have enjoyed your trip through time on the Western Branch of the Lynnhaven and its tributaries, coves, and small creeklets. You have traveled along the routes that are sites from Native American and colonial history through the developments of the 21st century. Your journey has revealed many changes in the landscape and waterways from the early days. The more we paddle and spend time near the water the more we realize that we need to care for the waters that connect us. We would like to leave you with this quote from the Mission Statement, the Third Canada's River Heritage Conference, which sums up our feelings.

> *Rivers connect us. They join us to our neighbors upstream and down. They link us to our past and to our future. Rivers are common bonds even where they form borders. Rivers give our lives a common purpose, which, in its best manifestations, translates into environmental and historical stewardship, and into art, music and literature.*

Essentials For Paddlers/Boaters

- PFD/Life jacket for every person in the craft
- Whistle attached to each life jacket
- Paddle (and a spare paddle if traveling alone in canoe or kayak)
- Water to drink
- Snacks, energy bars
- Bilge Pump or sponge
- Spray Skirt (if kayaking)
- First Aid Kit (also, see Safety list)
- Compass and map or chart

This is just a suggested list. Never forget that good, old common sense goes a long way to having fun on the water. Plan for the unexpected. Chance favors the prepared.

What To Wear?

- **Synthetics** dry quicker than cotton. Dress for the weather and always be prepared to get wet.
- Shoes? **Water sandals** are fine; flip-flops come off too easily. In cool weather wetsuit booties feel great.
- A **hat** with a brim, **sunglasses** and **sun block** will round out your paddling wardrobe.
- In cool weather, a **change of clothing** is a must. Be sure it's in a waterproof pouch. Cold weather paddling requires that a paddler be trained, in good physical shape, and dressed for the weather.

For more information, consult the American Canoe Association (ACA) website: *www.acanet.org*.

Boating Safety

- Pack **snacks and water**. No alcohol.

- You might want to stay out longer than you planned. Leave a **float plan**. Let someone know where you're headed and when you expect to return. Don't forget to call when you do return.

- In warm weather, bring **insect repellant** just in case.

- A **cell phone** (turned off!) in a proper waterproof container, not just a plastic bag, is a good idea in case you need something.

- **Check the tide** times before you launch. Many of these areas outside of the dredged channels are shallow at low tide and it can be a muddy walk back to your starting point.

- Nothing replaces good judgment and **proper training**. Take a course from a qualified paddling instructor, paddling school, or Coast Guard instructors.

- Bring **extra gasoline** if motorboating.

- Bring a **flashlight** or signaling device.

Note: This information is offered for guidance only and should not substitute for proper training and instruction. Water and air temperature need to be considered when making any trip by water. The authors assume no liability or risk for participation in watersports by the readers.

More Information

For a map and informational brochure of the **land portion of the Bayside History Trail**, contact the Virginia Beach Department of Parks and Recreation by telephone at (757) 427-4261 or e-mail: **fun@vbgov.com**.

Request *Bayside History Trail, Legacy on the Lynnhaven.*

It should be noted that these city sponsored projects began with citizen initiative. In 1994 Steve Hawthorne, then president of Pembroke Meadows and Shores Civic League came up with the idea of linking Bayside's historic sites through a bicycle or driving trail. With the help of the City of Virginia Beach, Departments of Libraries, Museum and Cultural Arts, and Parks and Recreation, the Bayside History Trail (by land) was dedicated on July 10, 1999, the date and time of the 293rd anniversary of Grace Sherwood's ducking in the Lynnhaven River.

References

Badger, Curtis J. 1996. *A Naturalist's Guide to the Virginia Coast.* Mechanicsburg, PA: Stackpole Books.

Barrow, Mary Reid. June 2, 1985. "German POWs Served Time on County's Farms," *The Beacon.* Norfolk, VA: Landmark Communications, Inc.

Barrow, Mary Reid. November 22, 1990. "A delicacy: oysters, shucked and fresh," *The Beacon.* Norfolk, VA: Landmark Communications, Inc.

Barrow, Mary Reid. March 8, 1998. "Shellfishing on the Lynnhaven was tradition as well as business," *The Beacon.* Norfolk, VA: Landmark Communications, Inc.

Barrow, Mary Reid. November 11, 1997. "Sonar hints at Thoroughgood's watery grave," *The Beacon.* Norfolk, VA: Landmark Communications, Inc.

Clark, Robert W. 1991. *A Map of Historic Sites in Princess Anne County in 1691, Superimposed Upon Modern Day Virginia Beach.* Virginia Beach, VA: CBN.

Crompton, John L. 2000. *The Impact of Parks and Open Space on Property Values and the Property Tax Base.* Ashburn, VA: National Recreation and Park Association.

de Gast, Robert. 1970. *The Oystermen of the Chesapeake.* Camden, Maine: International Publishing Company.

Egloff, Keith and Woodward, Deborah. 1992. *First People: The Early Indians of Virginia,* Richmond, Virginia: The Virginia Department of Historic Resources.

Editor, The Friends of Ferry Plantation House. Summer, 1998. "Ferry's Story Told," *Ferry Tidings.* Virginia Beach, VA: Friends of Ferry Plantation House.

Fairlamb, Sadler & Whitehead Architects, P.C. and Burkhart/Thomas Architecture•Interior Design. 1996. *A Study of The Ferry Plantation House.*

Flachsenhaar, Mary. August 13, 1995. "The Old-fashioned Way," *The Virginian-Pilot and the Ledger-Star.* Norfolk, VA: Landmark Communications, Inc.

Fleet, Beverley. 1988. *Virginia Colonial Abstracts.* Baltimore, MD: Genealogical Publishing Co., Inc.

Forrest, William S. 1853. *Historical and Descriptive Sketches of Norfolk and Vicinity.* Philadelphia, PA: Lindsay and Blakiston.

Hampton Roads Chamber of Commerce. 1999. *This Is Hampton Roads.* Norfolk, VA: Amy G. Bull.

Hawkins-Hendrix, Edna. 1998. *Black History Our Heritage: Princess Anne County, Virginia Beach, Virginia, A Pictorial History,* Virginia Beach,VA: self-published.

Keeling, John W. November, 2002. Personal Communication.

Kyle, Louisa Venable. July 15, 1956. "Up the Lynnhaven: Nature's Pageant Today Prompts Memories of River Life Yesterday," *The Virginian-Pilot,* Norfolk, VA: Landmark Communications, Inc.

Kyle, Louisa Venable. 1964. *Tidewater Virginia in Years Gone By,* Second Edition. Norfolk, VA: Mutual Federal Savings and Loan Association of Norfolk.

Kyle, Louisa Venable. 1969. *The History of the Eastern Shore Chapel and Lynnhaven Parish.* Norfolk, VA: Teagle and Little, Inc.

Lester, Calvert. December 10, 2002. Personal Communication.

Mansfield, Steven S. 1989. *Princess Anne County and Virginia Beach, A Pictorial History.* Norfolk, VA: The Donning Company.

Mason, George Carrington, editor. 1949. *The Colonial Vestry Book of Lynnhaven Parish, Princess Anne County, Virginia, 1723-1786*. Newport News, VA: self-published.

McCrary, Ben C. 1995. *Indians in Seventeenth Century Virginia*. Baltimore, MD: Genealogical Publishing Company, Inc.

McIntosh, Charles F. 1924. "Saunders- Princess Anne County, Virginia," *The Virginia Magazine of History and Biography*, Volume 32. Richmond, VA: Old Dominion Press, Inc.

Meade, William. 1857. *Old Churches, Ministers, and Families of Virginia*, Volume I. Philadelphia, PA: J.B. Lippincott & Company.

Meyer, Virginia and Dorman, John, editors. 1987. *Adventurers of Purse and Person*. Richmond, VA: Dietz Press.

Nash, Belinda. June 2000. "Step Into The Past 'Down on the Lynnhaven.' " *Ferry Tidings*. Virginia Beach, VA: Friends of Ferry Plantation House.

Norfolk Museum Bulletin. March, 1961. "Thoroughgood House Gift," Norfolk, VA: The Norfolk Museum.

Nugent, Nell Marion. 1992. *Cavaliers and Pioneers, Abstracts of Virginia Land Patents and Grants*, Volume I, 1623-1666. Richmond, VA: Virginia State Library.

Nugent, Nell Marion. 1977. *Cavaliers and Pioneers, Abstracts of Virginia Land Patents and Grants*, Volume II. Richmond, VA: Virginia State Library.

Rountree, Helen C. 1996. *Pocahontas's People, The Powhatan Indians of Virginia Through Four Centuries*. Norman, OK: University of Oklahoma Press.

Tazewell, C. W., editor. 1991. *Where the Wild Goose Goes: B. D. White, Preservationist*. Virginia Beach, VA: W. S. Dawson Company.

Tazewell, C. W., editor. 1991. *Virginia Beach Vibes: More People and Hogs*. Virginia Beach, VA: W. S. Dawson Company.

Tazewell, William L. and Friddell, Guy. 2000. *Norfolk's Waters: An Illustrated History of Hampton Roads*. Sun Valley, CA: American Historical Press.

Virginia Beach Public Library. 1996. *The Beach*. Virginia Beach, VA: Department of Public Libraries, City of Virginia Beach.

Waugaman, Sandra & Moretti-Langholtz, Danielle. 2000. *We're Still Here: Contemporary Virginia Indians Tell Their Stories*. Richmond, VA: Palari Publishing.

Walke, Henry. circa 1890. *Brief Records and Recollections: Private Record of Walke Family in the United States*.

Whichard, Rogers Dey. 1959. *The History of Lower Tidewater Virginia*, Volume I, New York: Lewis Publishing Company, Inc.

White, Benjamin Dey. 1924. *Gleanings in the History of Princess Anne County*. Princess Anne County, VA: self-published.

Helpful Resources

Adam Thoroughgood House
1636 Parish Road
Virginia Beach, VA 23455
757-460-7588

American Canoe Association (ACA)
7432 Alban Station Blvd B-22
Springfield, VA 22150-2311
703-451-0141
www.acanet.org

American Rivers
1430 Vermont Avenue NW, Suite 720
Washington, DC 20005-3516
202-347-9224
www.amrivers.org

Association for the Preservation of Virginia Antiquities (APVA)
204 West Franklin Street
Richmond, VA 23220-5021

Chesapeake Bay Foundation
Virginia Office
Capital Place
1108 E. Main Street, Suite 1600
Richmond, VA 23219
804-780-1392
www.savethebay.cbf.org

Chrysler Museum of Art
245 West Onley Road
Norfolk, VA 23507
757-664-6200

Clean Water Network
1200 New York Avenue NW, Suite 400
Washington, DC 20005
202-289-2395
www.cwn.org

The Conservation Fund
1800 N Kent Street, Suite 1120
Arlington, VA 22209-2109

Department of Conservation and Recreation
203 Governor Street, Suite 206
Richmond, VA 23219-2094
804-796-1712
www.dcr.state.va.us

Department of Game and Inland Fisheries
4010 West Broad Street
Richmond, VA 23230
804-367-1000
www.dgif.state.va.us

Department of Historic Resources
2801 Kensington Avenue
Richmond, VA 23221
804-367-2391

Friends of Ferry Plantation House, Inc.
4136 Cheswick Lane
Virginia Breach, VA 23455
757-473-5626

Friends of Lynnhaven House
4401 Wishart Lane
Virginia Breach, VA 23455
757-460-1688

Leave No Trace
P.O. Box 997
Boulder, CO 80306
303-442-8222
www.LNT.org

Morning Star Baptist Church
4800 First Court Road
Virginia Beach, VA 23455
757-464-3663

National Audubon Society
P.O. Box 52529
Boulder, CO 80322
800-274-4201

National Register of Historic Places
National Park Service,
Mid-Atlantic Regional Office
143 South Third Street
Philadelphia, PA 19106
215-597-7995

The Nature Conservancy
Virginia Chapter
490 Westfield Road
Charlottesville, VA 22901
804-295-6106
www.nature.org

North American Water Trails
56 Pease Road
Appleton, ME 04862-6455
207-785-4079

Princess Anne County/Virginia Beach Historical Society
Upper Wolfsnare Plantation
2040 Potters Road
Virginia Beach, VA 23454
757-491-3490

Virginia Beach Department of Parks and Recreation
2408 Courthouse Drive, Building 21
Virginia Beach, VA 23456-9016
757-563-1100

Virginia Beach Historical Register
Department of Museums and Cultural Arts
3131 Virginia Beach Blvd
Virginia Beach, VA 23452
757-431-4000

Virginia Beach Visitor's Center
2100 Parks Avenue
Virginia Beach, VA 23451
800-822-3224
www.vbfun.com

Virginia Professional Paddlesports Assn
7432 Alban Station Blvd B-22
Springfield, VA 22150-2311
703-451-3864
www.propaddle.com

Index

Adam Thoroughgood Foundation, 52
Adam Thoroughgood House, 9
Alfriend, Richard, 62
Algonquian, 23
Anthony Walke Tavern, 64
Apasus, 24
Asheville Bridge Creek, 57
Asheville Creek, 57

Baptismal Font, 43
Barnett Family, 48
Bayberry Candles, 25
Bayside, 52, 67
Bayside History Trail, 8, 58, 61
Bayside History Trail, Land Portion, 83
Bayville Dairy Farms, 35
Bayville Golf Club, 35, 37
Bayville Manor, 26, 37, 41
Bennett, Joane, 70
Bennett, Samuell, 70-71
Bennetts Creek, 69
Berkeley, William, 19
Birds, 24
  game, 25
  nesting, 24
Boating Safety, 82
Boush Family, 59
Broad Bay, 23
Broad Creek, 19
Broadwater, John, 62
Buchannan Creek, 64, 69

Camp Ashby, 75, 78
Camp Thalia, 78
Cannons, Signal, 66
Canoe/Kayak Access, 30
Cape Henry, 16, 40
Charles River County, 70
Chesapeake, 16
Chesapeake Bay, 16, 18, 21, 27, 31, 53
Chesapeake Bay Foundation, 35, 40

Chesapeans, 23, 24, 25
  fishing, 23
  subsistence, 24, 25
  villages, 24
Chief Powhatan, 23
Chief Seattle, 68
Church Point, 21, 42, 47, 50, 51, 62, 63
Colonial Williamsburg Foundation, 64
Courthouse(s), 19, 53, 58, 64, 42
  Church Point, 42
  Elizabeth River, 19
  Ferry Farm, 20
  Princess Anne Road, 44
  Wolfsnare Creek, 19
Crab Creek, 18, 34, 68
Crops, 26, 68

Dickson, Robert, 61
Donation Farm, 61

Ebenezer Methodist Episcopal Church South, 58
Elizabeth City Shire, 19, 44, 70
Elizabeth River, 19, 46, 66
Ellegood, John, 76

Farrer, John, 19
Farrer, Virginia, 19
Ferries, 11, 65, 66
Ferry Plantation, 43, 74, 66
Ferry Plantation House, 44, 48, 57, 58, 64, 65
First Landing State Park, 23
Flat-bottom Boats, 27

Garrison Plantation, 41
Gaskin, Savill, 59, 65
Glebe Lands, 21
Glebes, 47
Gookin, Daniel, 52
Gookin, John, 52, 53
Gookin, Sarah, 53, 76

Haines, John, 60
Hampton Roads, 8, 44
Hariot, Thomas, 24
Hawthorne, Steve, 83
Haygood Chapel, 58
Haygood Methodist Memorial, 58
Haygood United Methodist Church, 58
Haygood, Atticus G., 58
Hebden Cove, 68
Hebden Family, 68
Honey, 25
Hunter, Robert R., 64

Indians, *See Native American*
   Chesapeake, 23
   oyster roast, 38
   Nanticoke, 23
Ivy League Academy Christian Learning Center, 77

John Gookin's Landing, 52-53

Keeling's Oyster Cove, 49
Keeling, Adam, 49
Keeling, John Wesley, 49
Keeling, Solomon Godfrey, 49
Kempe's Landing, 44
Kicotan, (Kecoughtan), 51
King Charles II, 25
Kyle, Louisa Venable, 57, 74

Lake Windsor, 71, 75
Lauraceous, 26
Leopold, Aldo, 45
Lesner Bridge, 18, 30, 31
Lesner, John A., 31
Linhaven River, 52
Linhaven Parish, 19
Little Creek, 16, 21
Little Neck, 47, 49, 68
   subdivisions, 48
Little Neck Point, 38
Logan, Charlie, 41
London Bridge, 21
London Company, 25

Louis, Madison, 41
Lynnhaven Bay, 16, 18, 19, 23, 40, 57
Lynnhaven Boat and Beach Facility, 18, 30
Lynnhaven Ferry System, 65
Lynnhaven Golf and Country Club, 73
Lynnhaven House, 59, 60, 65
Lynnhaven Inlet, 21, 27
Lynnhaven Parish, 51, 61
Lynnhaven Parish Church, 61, 62, 63
Lynnhaven River, 16, 19, 20, 21, 23, 25, 38, 43, 44, 46, 53, 55, 57, 58, 59, 63, 64, 65, 68, 69, 70
   log bridge, 48
Lynnhaven Roads, 8

Marine Sonics Technology, 62
McDonald, James, 53
McIntosh Bridge, 72
McIntosh, Charles, 64
McIntosh, George, 64, 74
Meade, William, 21
Monitor National Marine Sanctuary, 62
Monitor Project, 62
Morning Star Baptist Church, 41
Mount Trashmore, 75
Mount Trashmore Park, 70, 71
Muddy Creek, 55, 57
Mulberry, White, 25

Nansemond County, 52, 69
Nash, Belinda, 57
National Oceanic Atmospheric Administration, 63
Native American, 8, 23, 24, 37, 68
   arrows and spears, 23
   projectile points, 23, 24
   trails, 8
New Town, 44
New World, 11, 19
Norfolk County, Lower, 19, 44

Norfolk County, New, 44
Norfolk County, Upper, 44
Norfolk, Lower, 19

Ocean Park Beach Area, 31
O'Keefe's Oyster Pavilion, 40
Offley, Sarah, 50, 76
Old Donation Church, 20, 42, 43, 44, 58, 61, 68
Oliver Family, 60
Oyster Gardener, 40
Oyster Roast, 38, 39, 49

Paddling Clothing, 81
Paddling Essentials, 80
Painter, Floyd, 20, 23
Pembroke, 76
Pembroke East Shoppes, 76
Pembroke Mall, 72, 76
Pembroke Manor House, 77
Pembroke Meadows and Shores Civic League, 83
Pembroke Plantation, 25, 77
Percy, George, 38
Phaneuf, Brett, 62
Pleasure House Beach, 34
Pleasure House Cove, 36
Pleasure House Creek, 34, 37, 42
Pleasure House Point, 34
Pleasure House Road, 34
Poquoson of York County, 69
Princess Anne, *See Queen Anne*
Princess Anne County, 16, 20, 27, 44, 45, 51, 56, 67, 68, 74
Princess Anne High School, 71, 76
Prisoner of War (POW) Camp, 75, 78
Pungo, 55

Queen Anne, 62

Rade D'Hampton, 8

S. G. Keeling Oyster Roast Restaurant, 49
Salgoff, Mark, 46
Salicornia, 25

Saltwort, *See Salicornia*
Samuell Bennetts Creek, 52, 69
Samuell Bennetts Plantation, 70
Sassafras, 26
Saunders, John, 25, 76
Scull Neck, 65
Sea Turtle, 36
Shallop, 9
Sherwood, Grace, 54, 55-58, 83
Silkworm, 25
Singleton, Peter, 37
Skiff, 9, 66, 74
Steinhilber's Thalia Acres Inn, 11, 73
Steinhilber, Robert, 73
Summerville Plantation, 72, 74
Swift, Jonathan, 38

Taft, President, 40
Tavern(s), 26, 53, 64
Thalia, 73, 75, 77
Thalia Creek, 69, 71, 72, 75
Thalia Elementary School, 71, 76
The Association for the Preservation of Virginia Antiquities, 60
The Mariners' Museum, 63
The Town Center, 72
The Witch of Pungo, 55, 57
Thelaball, Francis, 59
Thoreau, Henry David, 20
Thoroughgood Cove, 50, 52
Thoroughgood, Adam, 37, 42, 50-52, 61, 66, 76, 70
Thoroughgood, Sarah, 52, 76
Thurston Branch, 52, 64, 69-71
Tidewater Victory Memorial Hospital, 78
Tiler, William, 70
Timber Necke, 76
Tobacco, 26, 46, 47, 56
Trading Point, 47
Transport Goods, *See Flat-bottom Boats*
Truck Farming, 27
Two Penny Point, 66

Virginia Beach Department of Parks and Recreation, 83
Virginia Beach, VA, 11, 23, 44, 45, 51, 77, 79
Virginia Company of London, 19
Virginia Institute of Marine Science, 35
Walke Manor House, 64
Walke, Elizabeth, 74
Walke, Henry, 43
Walke, William, 54
Washington, George, 59
Waxmyrtle, 25
Wetmore, Lansing D., 41
White Acres, 67
White, Benjamin Dey, 62, 67, 68
White, Elisha, 41
White, John, 24, 56
William Walke Manor House, 44
Willis Furniture, 78
Windmill, 54, 74
  uses, 54
Wishart House, 59
Witch Duck Bay, 54, 57, 67, 69
Witch Duck Point, 18, 54, 55, 57, 67
Witch Ducking Trial, 56
Wolfsnare Creek, 19, 44
World War II, 75, 78

Yeardley, Francis, 76
Yeardley, George, 76
York County, 70

About the Authors

Lillie Gilbert has been a resident of Virginia Beach, VA since 1967. She received a BA in English Literature from Queens College and an MA from the College of William and Mary. Lillie taught for 17 years in the Virginia Beach City Public Schools and is currently the owner of Wild River Outfitters. A former canoe racer, she is a canoe and kayak guide for Wild River Outfitters Touring Company, LLC. Actively involved in environmental affairs, Lillie serves as a volunteer for the Virginia Beach Department of Parks and Recreation, Earth Day events, and Clean the Bay Day events. She has been instrumental in helping to establish the city's Scenic Waterway System and the "Adopt-A-Waterway" program.

Belinda Nash is a Canadian who moved to Virginia Beach, VA in the early 1980s. Intrigued by the history of the area that has become her home, the local folklore has become dear to her. While doing research, inconsistencies in local history had revealed that more research was necessary, especially on Grace Sherwood, The Witch of Pungo. Belinda interprets the life and times of Grace Sherwood at Virginia Beach's historic Ferry Plantation House, local schools, and various civic events. She is currently at work on a biography about Virginia's only convicted witch that was tried by water. Belinda is a member of the Board of Directors of Ferry Plantation House, treasurer of the Pembroke Meadows/ Shores Civic League Association, and historian at Old Donation Church. She has three children: Kimberley, Donovan, and Danielle, and granddaughter Kathlene. Belinda is married to Herbert Nash and has three step children: Michael, Douglas and Scott, and three grandchildren: Amber, David and Jordan.

Deni Norred-Williams has resided in Virginia Beach, VA since 1988. She received a BA degree in Special Education from James Madison University and an Educational Specialist